EXTREME CAREERS

SCUBA DIVERS

Life Under Water

John Giacobello

the rosen publishing group's
rosen
central

Published in 2001 by The Rosen Publishing Group, Inc.
29 East 21st Street, New York, NY 10010

First Edition

Library of Congress Cataloging-in-Publication Data

Giacobello, John.
Scuba divers : life under water / by John Giacobello. — 1st ed.
p. cm. — (Extreme Careers)
Includes bibliographical references (p.) and index.
ISBN 0-8239-3368-7
1. Scuba diving—Vocational guidance—Juvenile literature.
[1. Scuba diving—Vocational guidance. 2. Vocational guidance.]
I. Title. II. Series
GV838.672 .G53 2001
797.2'3—dc21
                                                      00-012608

Manufactured in the United States of America

Contents

Take the Plunge

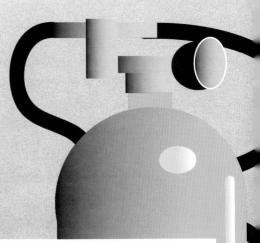

Few places are more extreme than the ocean. It's huge, covering over 70 percent of the planet. It's mysterious, containing life-forms and sunken artifacts waiting to be discovered. It's filled with hidden dangers, like powerful currents, intense water pressure, and deadly marine life. Life fills the ocean bottom to top, from tiny shrimp and plankton to enormous humpback whales. No wonder many people call the ocean our planet's final frontier.

Imagine floating weightlessly through a bed of waving seaweed, as bright orange and yellow fish glide by overhead. The sun streams down and you dive to the sandy ocean floor to examine a glistening glass object. All is quiet and serene. Suddenly, you are startled by a gigantic, bug-eyed, sharp-spined fish! Since you cannot identify the creature, you stay completely still as it swims toward you. It darts away as rapidly as it appeared, and you breathe a sigh of relief.

It is this combination of serenity and thrilling discovery that draws curious explorers to the deep blue sea. With masks on their faces and fins on their feet, divers often look like some sort of frogmen straight out of a science fiction movie.

The equipment a diver uses to breathe under water is called a self-contained underwater breathing apparatus (SCUBA). Some divers get their oxygen from tanks strapped to their backs, while others are attached to hoses that lead to larger tanks kept on ships.

So how did we ever come up with this strange idea? Why did anyone ever decide to try breathing through a tube to stay under water? Mankind has always been fascinated with the sea. Some people say that all life began there and that somewhere, deep inside, we remember it as home. This may be one reason we are drawn to bodies of water. Another could be mystery. For the same reasons astronauts are compelled to shoot into space to explore the outer limits, divers are drawn to the lure of unknown underwater worlds.

Testing
the Waters

One of the first designs for a diving apparatus was created in 1680 by Italian physicist Giovanni Alfonzo Borelli. Some of his ideas, like using a breathing tube to connect a diving suit and helmet to an airbag, influenced future designs for diving gear. But Borelli's helmet and airbag were made of leather. If anyone had ever actually tried out his designs, they would have drowned almost immediately!

In 1772, a Frenchman named Sieur Freminet had some success with a leather diving suit, a copper helmet, and a container of compressed air. The container was connected to a larger tank on the boat. Freminet went down as far as fifteen meters and performed several successful dives. The dives lasted

only a few minutes but were considered revolution-
ary at the time.

By 1832, after much experimentation by other
diving pioneers, divers were staying under water
twenty-five to thirty minutes at a time. In 1865, two
Frenchmen named Benoit Rouquayrol and Auguste
Denayrouze made greater improvements to the basic
diving suit, which allowed the diver to disconnect
from the larger air tank for short periods of time. By

A scuba diver models a re-creation of the diving suit
that Rouquayrol and Denayrouze invented in 1865.

1923, a suit that resisted water pressure down to 160 meters deep was developed. The problem with this suit was that it was huge and it made movement difficult. A diver wearing the suit resembled a man made of white, puffy marshmallows.

Technology has enabled diving suits and gear to slim down considerably since the 1920s. Today's equipment is lightweight and effective and is tested to meet the most rigorous safety standards. Because of the easy availability of safe diving gear today, an activity that was once the strict territory of scientists is practiced by thrill seekers from every walk of life. Anyone in good health can receive the necessary training to comfortably glide along the ocean floor, as inventors of the past could only dream of doing.

As a result, a whole new range of job possibilities has opened up for those seeking an extreme career. There are many tasks that need to be accomplished in our oceans, lakes, and rivers, and people are needed to jump in and get to work. For example, ships sometimes sink and, when they do, the world wants details. We need to find out what happened, why it happened, and exactly who and what are down there. Valuables need to be transported to the surface and any hazardous materials need to be cleared out of the water.

Professional divers take pictures of the undersea world so we can all appreciate its beauty and mystery. They make underwater adventure films possible. They find relics of lost civilizations. They help convict criminals by finding lost evidence, play vital roles in military operations, and guide sport divers on unforgettable adventures. And that barely scratches the surface of what professional divers accomplish every day. A diving career offers extreme thrills and chills to those who follow its watery path, and those who follow that path make extremely important contributions to the rest of us.

Swimming to Work

So what exactly do professional divers do? There are opportunities for them in the recreational dive industry, journalism, movies, medicine, the military, and more. The following are some underwater careers that continue to grow in popularity.

Resort Dive Guide

As scuba grows as a hobby, more and more people choose to vacation at dive resorts. These are lush, tropical havens where divers can go on guided diving expeditions. It is the job of the resort dive guide to lead those expeditions and to help make them as safe and fun as possible.

The best part about being a resort dive guide is that the guide gets to do his or her job in an underwater paradise. Some obstacles that guides can run into include the breakdown of equipment, illness or serious panic among the group's divers, or divers lying about their level of experience and getting themselves into hot water. The guide must be well trained to handle any problem that rises to the surface.

Dive Instructor

Dive instructors teach people the necessary skills of diving: how to use the equipment, how to breathe properly under water, and how to execute a dive without ending up an oceanic casualty. They also generate excitement about diving. Instructors should be able to open students' eyes to the adventure and romance of exploring underwater worlds.

A dive instructor shows his scuba students how to give the diver's hand signal for "OK."

The dive instructor must also be a highly responsible individual. Getting into deep water with beginner or first-time divers means taking the lives of others into one's own hands. An instructor must do everything in his or her power to ensure the safety of the students during classes. He or she must also teach students how to remain responsible for their own safety long after training has finished.

Diving Journalist, Underwater Photographer, and Underwater Cinematographer

The ocean is a big part of our popular culture. Suspenseful movies, colorful photographs, and fascinating stories bring the beauty and danger of the sea to life for all of us. We watch television specials that portray the adventures of scuba divers while at the same time teach us about undersea animal and plant life.

The people who bring us these images and information are diving journalists, underwater photographers, and underwater cinematographers. Diving journalists and underwater photographers are usually the same people. They come up with hot ideas for diving-related magazines like *Scuba Times*, *Diver*, and *Skin Diver*. They sometimes write and photograph for mainstream magazines, too.

These journalists may dive to photograph remains of shipwrecks, sunken treasures or artifacts, or rare

In this underwater photo, a scuba-diving cinematographer films kelp.

underwater life-forms. They then write about their experiences, along with background information they have researched. Diving journalists must be able to capture the intensity and emotion of their dives to engage readers. They may also take photos for advertisements, resort brochures, or books like this one.

Underwater cinematographers can work on many different kinds of projects, from educational television shows to blockbuster Hollywood movies. Films like *Deep Blue Sea* and *Jaws* rely heavily on divers skilled at filming action sequences under water. Usually the sharks and other dangerous creatures used in these films are robots or animated images. But sometimes the cameraperson is asked to find real, and often deadly, undersea animals to film. He or she may even have to agitate the animals to get them to perform for the camera!

Diver Medic and Diver Physician

Diver medics and physicians exist because diving injuries are unique. Say a diver comes out of the water with intense pain in her ears, dizzy and unable to hear properly. Or someone is writhing in agony with a sharp sea urchin spine lodged in his leg and a fever coming on. Would your average family physician know how best to treat these problems? Probably not.

That's why the diving community needs specialized health care. Diver medics can be on hand to administer first aid and CPR when something goes wrong at a dive site. The medic, who does not have training as advanced as a medical doctor's, can aid the patient until he or she can be transported to the diver physician's office. Sometimes, physicians will come to the site to help the patient. Both diver physicians and diver medics are highly skilled and knowledgeable about specific health problems that divers encounter.

Salvage Diver

Ever dream about diving for sunken treasure? Would you love to go on an adventurous hunt for silver bars and gold coins in wooden chests? It sounds like a fantasy, but there are divers who make their living seeking out sunken ships and the riches they some-times hold. One such ship was the Spanish *Nuestra Señora de Atocha*, which sank somewhere in the Florida Keys in 1622. An American salvage diver named Mel Fisher, whose diving crew included many family members, had spent seventeen years studying maps and documents from the seventeenth century. Finally, in 1985, he found the ship, which housed artifacts and valuables totaling around $400 million! The price of success was high, however. Time, money, and even human lives—including Fisher's son—were lost along the way.

Besides searching for lost ships from past centuries, salvage divers make a great deal of their income recovering cargo from vessels more recently sunk. They are also hired to remove hazardous chemicals that are accidentally dropped in the water or have gone down with a ship.

In addition to exceptional diving skills, powerful and expensive equipment is needed to recover heavy cargo from the ocean floor. Dangers include collapsing ship walls, poor visibility, and becoming trapped in a vessel. Sometimes, salvage can be

Underwater archaeologists help recover valuable artifacts from sunken ships for scientific and historical study.

simply routine, but it can also be romantic and exciting. After all, it was salvage divers who found and photographed the most famous shipwreck in history, the legendary *Titanic*.

Underwater Archaeologist

Underwater archaeology is similar to salvage diving in that it involves hunting for shipwrecks. The difference is the reason for doing it. Salvage diving is usually done to recover something of value, while archaeological dives are executed in the name of scientific study. Shipwrecks can teach us about a historical incident or aspects of a certain culture. They act as underwater time capsules.

Underwater archaeologists also explore areas that were once lands populated by people and are now submerged because the ocean's water level has risen over time. In underwater caves, they find ceremonial statues, ancient skeletons, and even human brain material from ages past!

Marine Biologist

Like an underwater archaeologist, a marine biologist also scuba dives in the name of scientific study. Rather than shipwrecks, however, the biologist studies sea life and how it fits into the entire marine environment. Marine biologists are also sometimes referred to as marine ecologists.

This strict scientific discipline seeks to answer questions such as "How do fish move through the water?" "How do they survive in salt water or freshwater?" "Which of their senses are developed?" "What is their position in the food chain?" The list goes on and on.

Learning about the life cycles of marine animals can help people improve underwater ecology. For instance, if an oil spill occurs in a particular area, scientists are able to predict how marine life—and, in turn, human life—will be affected. Biologists have also discovered nutritious food and vital drugs in the sea, and have even learned to raise underwater crops.

Perhaps most important, we can all make greater efforts to protect the marine ecosystem by learning which species are becoming endangered and why. Knowing the specific consequences of harming our oceans makes many people reconsider bad habits, such as polluting and overfishing.

Police Search-and-Recovery Teams

Thanks to today's scuba search-and-recovery teams, crime evidence that was once considered lost is often found and, in turn, more crimes are solved. This kind of diving requires a great deal of courage, not to mention a strong stomach. Police divers must be able to recover corpses, or sometimes even just body parts. Imagine how difficult it would be to discover the body of a small child. Other responsibilities may include recovering a crashed airplane, checking out a shark scare, or scanning an area for bombs.

Diving in the Military

Professional divers play an important role in keeping our navy safe and strong. Who else would be able to perform repair and maintenance tasks on ships below the surface of the water? They also deal with naval rescue and salvage, as well as underwater construction. Some military divers are trained to specialize in finding and defusing underwater explosives, like missiles and bombs. This is one of the most high-pressure diving occupations. The diver's life and the lives of many others are in jeopardy if he or she does not keep a cool head and have nerves of steel when dealing with explosives.

This is just a sampling of the extreme careers available in the field of scuba diving. There are also bell saturation divers, who sink to great depths inside atmospherically controlled metal objects. Remotely operated vehicle (ROV) technicians operate underwater robotics. Commercial air divers

These divers are part of a U.S. Navy team that is mapping the wreckage of the Civil War–era ship *USS Monitor.*

perform underwater repairs, inspections, and construction tasks on oil rigs and bridges. These divers all risk injury and even death every time they go to work, and they are rewarded with careers that could never be described as dull!

Dangers Pro Divers Face

The ocean is an extremely foreign world to humans. Although many divers claim to feel a vague sense of familiarity even on their first underwater excursion, the depths of the sea will never truly be our turf. Since divers are strangers exploring an environment that they are not designed to survive in, there will always be an element of risk involved in a diving career. What follows are intense but true stories about specific dangers.

The Dreaded Shark Attack

While most people immediately think of shark attacks as the biggest threat to underwater safety, the truth is that sharks very rarely attack people. If a shark comes too close to a diver, a sharp punch in the nose is usually enough to discourage the beast. The image of the man-hunting, evil shark seeking out humans to mangle exists only in our popular imagination. Still, sharks sometimes do go after divers. And when they do, it is not pretty, as one survivor learned during the horrifying ordeal of a great white attack.

The survivor's name is Marco, and he owns a company that produces oceanographic equipment. Before his encounter, Marco was a very experienced diver who had no fear of the many sharks he had seen on the job. He understood how rare attacks were.

One day he was diving with some friends near a popular site. After going down about fifteen meters, he caught a glimpse of a gigantic fin to his right. He turned and saw a great white shark swimming away from him. Marco was excited to have actually seen a great white, but he also became a little nervous. He decided to get up to the boat so he could warn his friends.

As Marco prepared for return, he felt a presence to his left. Turning his head, he saw an enormous open mouth full of razor-sharp teeth racing toward him.

Before Marco could fully grasp what was happening, he realized he was being pulled through the water. The great white's jaws were clamped around his waist like a vise! Marco could feel intense pressure, but his metal equipment prevented serious cutting. The taste of metal is probably what caused the shark to spit out his prey and swim away.

The first thing Marco did was feel his legs to make sure they were still there. They were! He made his way back to the boat using an underwater scooter. It was a two-minute ride with poor visibility, and all the while he was terrified that the shark would return. When Marco surfaced near the boat, he

Scuba divers have to watch out for great white sharks like this one!

swam to it as quickly as possible. With all of his equipment weighing him down, he was in too much pain to get onto the boat so he just let the equipment go. Finally, he made it on board and leaned over the side to grab the abandoned gear. This caused him to fall back into the water!

Horrified, he scrambled up the ladder again. When his friends surfaced, they rushed the boat to shore and called an ambulance. Marco came out of the attack with some stitches and a mild fever, which are extremely light injuries for a great white attack. As soon as the cuts healed and the infection cleared up, he bravely went back into the water to do his job.

Choppy Waters and Strong Currents

Divers need to be extremely wary of water conditions. If the surface appears choppy and a strong current can be felt when entering the water, diving could be dangerous. One couple tells a story about being swept out to sea while foolishly diving in poor conditions.

Tony and Jennifer were on a dive boat with an inattentive guide. As soon as the boat anchored, the guide disappeared down the side with another diver. Tony and Jennifer realized the water looked pretty choppy, but they wanted to get their money's worth from the dive. So Jennifer jumped in.

Immediately, she was grasped by the current and swept far away from the boat. She could not swim back to it. Tony jumped in to help her and soon they were both drifting. Not only were they afraid of getting lost at sea with nobody to help them, but they had heard reports of a nine-foot shark harassing a fishing boat earlier that day. Soon, Tony began taking in too much water from being tossed around on the ocean's surface. He became very nauseated. They both decided it might be better to dive to the bottom and try to walk toward the boat.

The current was not as strong at the bottom. Still, trudging along was difficult, and they used up a lot of air. When Tony and Jennifer came up again, they were still quite far from the boat and once again caught in the current. They were near a reef, but they cut their hands while trying to hold on to it. And there were "old wives"—fish with poisonous dorsal fin spines—swimming all around them.

The couple inflated their "safety sausage," a bright, hot dog–shaped object that draws attention in emergencies, and were spotted by a fishing boat. But before the boat made it over to the couple, Tony began to drown. Because he had inhaled so much water, he was not getting enough oxygen into his system. When the boat was close enough, the skipper jumped into the water and helped them both on board. Tony and Jennifer survived the ordeal, a little wiser for the wear.

The Bends

"The bends" refers to the agonizing, sometimes deadly, condition that occurs when divers fail to rise slowly enough to the surface of the water. Why

Scuba divers returning from an archaeological site stop at a
ten-foot decompression point to avoid getting the bends.

do the bends happen? As divers swim deeper and deeper beneath the water's surface, their bodies absorb more and more nitrogen. This nitrogen gets pulled into the bloodstream when divers rise to the surface too quickly and nitrogen bubbles lodge in their joints, causing great pain. The bends can result in permanent health problems, even paralysis or death. Many divers consider the bends to be the biggest risk they face.

The answer to avoiding the bends is surfacing slowly, so that the nitrogen can work its way out of the body. Divers who swim to great depths must also practice "decompression diving." This involves pausing at certain depths on the way to the surface, to outgas the nitrogen. Some divers panic, or simply forget, and propel themselves upward like rockets. One man in southern California recalls a severe case of the bends he witnessed on a dive.

He noticed another diver in his group swimming upward at a rapid pace. When the diver reached the surface of the water, several people watched his eyes glaze over. He was pulled onto a boat and given oxygen. The diver was conscious but not responsive, and the right side of his body was not working properly. He appeared to be having a stroke.

A Coast Guard helicopter arrived within minutes. The diver was hauled up in a basket and taken to a decompression chamber. A decompression chamber is a small room where divers have simulated seawater pressure applied to their bodies, then are very slowly decompressed the way they should have been when they were in the water. After a few hours in the chamber, the diver was fine.

Illness

Do not swim with a cold. One diver who tried it swears "Never again." She had been ill, but she was slightly recovered and really wanted to dive. So she did. After going down about eight feet, her left ear cleared while the right one stayed badly clogged. At thirteen feet she heard an intense "POP!" and felt a sharp, stabbing pain in her nose and right ear. She was in such pain that she had trouble getting to the surface, which panicked her. When she finally made it, she could barely see and was completely disoriented. Fortunately, she was with her husband, who helped her to shore.

Her doctor reassured her that her eardrum was inflamed, but still intact. His diagnosis was that mucus, which had built up during her illness, probably loosened in the water and hit her eardrum. That was what caused the intense pain. Now, when she gets sick, this diver stays out of the water.

Irresponsible Dive Buddy

To help ensure safety, divers are warned to always dive with a buddy. In professional or sport diving, it is part of diver etiquette to help look out for one another under the water. Unfortunately, some divers forget about this important custom and become irresponsible.

One man went on a dive with a group of people he did not know, so he was assigned a buddy who was also there alone. The plan was for the group to gather at a sand patch after jumping off the boat. They would then swim off and explore the area together. The diver with the assigned buddy had an equipment problem before leaving the boat, so he reached the sand patch a few minutes late.

When he arrived, the group was gone. He was angry that his buddy did not tell them to wait. Since he already knew the area from previous dives, he caught up with the group in about ten minutes. Later he found out that his buddy did not even realize he was missing. If he had become lost or hurt, he would have had nobody to help him.

Other Threats to Underwater Safety

Some other problems divers report include equipment failure, hypothermia (low body temperature) in extremely cold water, and a strange kind of illness known as "rapture of the deep," which happens to deep sea divers who go down around ninety feet or more. Symptoms can include drowsiness, loss of motor skills, nausea, and impaired judgment. Rapture of the deep can also bring about a euphoric feeling, which is where the "rapture" part comes from.

Many divers seem to suffer a type of impaired judgment that is a function of their own egos. "The rules don't pertain to me." "I don't have to follow the dive plan." "I don't need special training; I can teach myself to deep sea dive." "I've never gone into a cave before, but how hard can it be?" And so on. These are the attitudes that create the worst risks of all for divers, professional or not. A poor attitude is a hundred times more dangerous than the most shark-infested waters.

Some problems are unavoidable. Who could foresee a mask being kicked off by another diver, or a lightning-fast shark attack out of nowhere? But there are different ways to respond to the unexpected, and many things divers can do before even getting into the water to minimize risk. We will talk about some of these safety strategies in the next chapter.

How Divers Avoid Tragedy

We've just looked at some of the horrifying things that can happen when people meet the sea. So is there any way to avoid tragedy when diving? What kinds of precautions do divers take to prevent underwater disasters from occurring?

Training

The most obvious key to diving safety is adequate training. While knowing the basic swimming strokes is not necessary for scuba diving, it is extremely helpful to feel comfortable in the water. Many divers have had at least some type of swimming lesson in the past. But believe it or not, some experienced divers— instructors even—cannot swim the length of a pool!

To be truly prepared for anything in diving, a diver must be trained by a responsible, knowledge-able, and capable instructor. This is one of the most important aspects of diving safety. A good instructor does not just teach the basic technical aspects of diving. He or she should also impart all of his or her

Students split classroom time with pool time while working toward their dive certification.

experience and wisdom to the students. Instructors should take responsibility for the safety of those they teach. To find a good instructor, you should interview candidates like a job recruiter would. You must find out details about the instructor's education, experience, specialties, interests, and goals.

Once you find an instructor, you must go through rigorous training in order to become certified as a diver. In order to legally set fin in the water without an instructor present, you must receive a "C-card" from a certifying agency. There are many different certifying agencies that provide both training and certification for diving students. Besides being certified, all divers should complete a rescue specialty course, which includes CPR and first-aid instruction.

Equipment

The importance of good equipment for divers cannot be stressed enough. Beneath the water, scuba gear is the only thing keeping a diver alive. Going out in

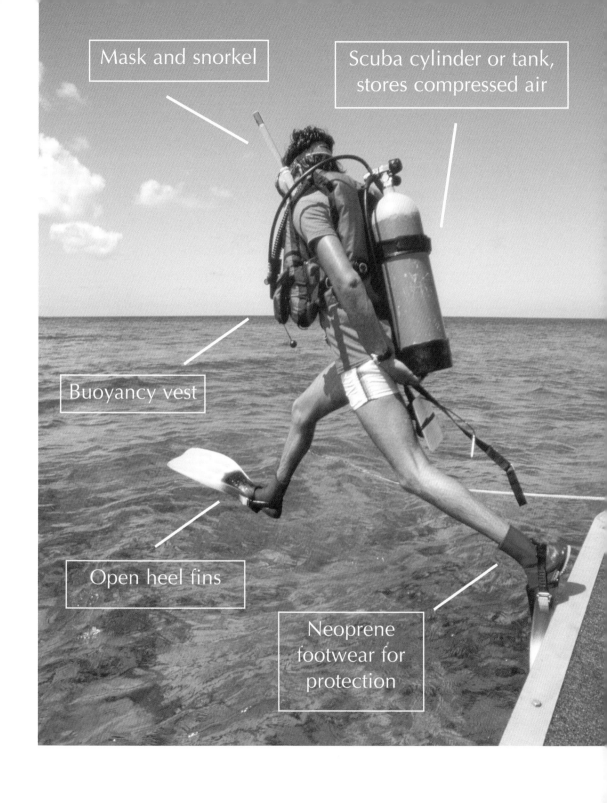

Mask and snorkel

Scuba cylinder or tank, stores compressed air

Buoyancy vest

Open heel fins

Neoprene footwear for protection

search of the cheapest gear available is a mistake divers often make. You must research the reputation of a gear manufacturer, talk to other divers and salespeople, then make a decision based on the information you have carefully gathered and reviewed.

No matter how expensive and trustworthy, all equipment must be inspected before every use. It can be helpful to have a buddy inspect your equipment as well. The air tank must be full, the weights used to control buoyancy must be free to drop at any time, and the regulator hose (the hose that connects your mouth with the tank) must be clear and correctly oriented. Everything from head to toe must be set up and functioning properly. The process does not take long, and it is a habit that can save lives.

Divers must always bring emergency equipment with them to the dive site. This includes a diving first-aid kit, a blanket, drinking water, and an oxygen delivery system. It is also important to have a communication device, such as a two-way radio or telephone, to call for help if necessary. Emergency phone numbers should be on hand so you can reach the Coast Guard, nearby hospitals, paramedics, or a decompression facility. The twenty-four-hour emergency number for the DAN (Divers Alert Network) is also invaluable for assisting in accidents. The number is listed at the back of this book.

The Diver's Worst Enemy: Panic

Diving can be stressful. When a diver feels tired, sick, cold, afraid, or disoriented, stress may result. For professional divers, there is also an element of job stress. This is okay, as long as the diver knows how to manage the stress. If he or she can remain calm when there are equipment malfunctions, shark threats, poor visibility, strong currents, or other underwater problems, manageable stress can provide energy and clarity to help the diver solve the problem. Divers who are well trained are generally good with stress. Because they are prepared to handle most any situation they encounter, they do not feel overwhelmed by unexpected occurrences.

But when stress becomes too great, it can lead to panic. Panic is one of the biggest threats to the life of a diver. Under water, panic almost always leads to injury or death. It makes thinking clearly and acting rationally nearly impossible. When problems occur, a diver must first control his or her breathing. Panic causes breathing to accelerate. In a diving situation, panicked breathing uses up a great deal of valuable air. Stressed divers may also begin to hyperventilate if they imagine they are not getting enough air from the tank. When breathing is under control, clear thinking resumes.

Managing the Unexpected

Problems that seem minor on the surface require extra care under the water. For example, coughing does not usually pose a threat to our well-being in day-to-day life. But when divers cough, they run the risk of inhaling water. Quickly swallowing several times usually solves that dilemma. Cramps can also become an issue for a diver. A sudden shooting pain may bring about panic in an underwater situation. The best solution is to have a buddy massage the cramp out.

As with many risky activities, planning and advance
preparation make scuba diving relatively safe.

Creating and Following a Dive Plan

As with many risky activities, good planning and
preparation make scuba diving safer. Professional
divers must prepare well in advance of going under
water to do their jobs. They must first be certain
they are in excellent health. Even the slightest hint of
a cold can cause major problems, as we read in the

previous chapter. They must also understand the climate of their dive site and have the appropriate equipment on hand. Weather conditions must be carefully considered, and storms or strong currents can force a diver to take the day off. Visibility and marine life common to the area should also be known before diving.

While training and preparation are vital aspects of diver safety, common sense plays a big role as well. For example, any diver who has earned a C-card knows how important it is to ascend to the surface slowly. Yet many ignore this most basic rule of thumb and end up with serious cases of the bends. Refraining from diving in bad weather or strong currents, always diving with a buddy, and avoiding quick movements around sharks are other common-sense practices often ignored. Thinking before acting usually keeps divers out of trouble.

Diving into the Future

W ith more and more people seeking careers and recreation under water, today's diving industry continues to grow by leaps and bounds. And so do advances in diving technology. Divers of the past would gasp at the array of gadgets and devices being developed for today's pro and sport divers. Things in the scuba world are getting downright James Bond!

Dive Computers

You probably would not jump into the Pacific Ocean with your PC or Mac strapped to your back. Yet many pro and sport divers are now using a new brand of compact, waterproof computer while submerged. These are called dive computers, and they make it easier for divers to avoid decompression problems like the bends.

These computers are programmed to detect water depth, time spent under water, and water temperature. With this information, they can calculate how many minutes can be safely spent at certain depths and how quickly the divers may ascend to the surface. All of these figures appear on gauges the diver must periodically check. If a diver begins surfacing too fast, the computer flashes a warning.

Hi-Tech Masks and Communication Devices

Diving masks have traditionally offered limited visibility. Divers could see only directly in front of themselves, and their downward vision was blocked by the bottom of the mask. A new mask has been developed that expands downward vision, allowing divers to read instruments and view other equipment below eye level. Special magnification lenses and prisms help to make details clearer and more readable. Even more futuristic is a new computerized mask, which displays readouts before the diver's eyes. This mask must be attached to the dive computer.

Underwater voice communication units, as shown in science fiction movies like *Sphere*, are not just figments

Underwater voice communication units, like this one from the movie *Sphere*, make it possible for divers to talk to one another under water.

of screenwriters' imaginations. While most divers must communicate using hand signals and gestures, those who can afford these expensive units can hold "deep" conversations. There are some problems associated with these items, however. Divers may communicate only within a certain range, and undersea obstacles like plants, bubbles, and temperature changes can prevent the devices from working properly.

Regulators

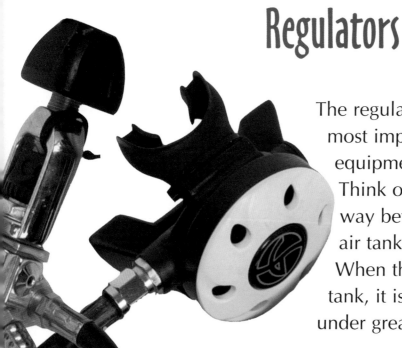

The regulator is one of the most important pieces of equipment a diver uses. Think of it as the doorway between the diver's air tank and mouth. When the air is in the tank, it is compressed and under great pressure. The

Without a regulator, divers cannot safely breathe compressed air from tanks.

regulator decreases that pressure to keep the air from shooting out of the tank and blowing a hole through the diver's esophagus!

Today's regulators are becoming as specialized as most other dive gadgets. A new cold-water regulator can continue to deliver air in spite of temperatures below forty degrees Fahrenheit. It also performs well in polluted areas. This can be very helpful for professional divers who may have to work in poor conditions. There are also special regulators to be used specifically for breathing nitrox, which is explained below.

Nitrox

In diving, nitrox refers to a special kind of air. When divers breathe nitrox from their tanks, they are taking in less nitrogen than they would with a normal air supply. Since decompression sickness is caused by absorption of nitrogen in the body, breathing in less nitrogen helps to avoid that problem. Divers breathing this chemical mixture can often dive deeper for longer periods of time.

Gadgets and gases are not the only ways that diving knowledge and understanding have increased over the years. We have made great strides in marine ecology, and the way that divers conduct themselves under the water has changed in the last three decades. Today, most divers follow a strict code of ethics when they are under the water. They approach diving very carefully and conservatively because they realize how little about this foreign land is truly understood. Also, we have effects on the underwater ecosystem without even realizing it.

For example, coral is very fragile. It has only a thin coating of protective mucus that keeps it from being damaged by the environment. In the past, divers did not realize they had to be careful about touching it. Now we know that just one touch could nearly destroy a piece of coral. Too many divers touching coral colonies could have long-term negative effects on the undersea environment.

This can apply to other marine life as well. Most divers today will not ride large fish or pick up snails because they do not know what kind of effect that could have on the animal or environment. Using food to attract fish is also a bad idea because it could disrupt the food chain.

A sense of responsibility toward themselves, other divers, and the marine environment is what allows divers to continue working and playing safely under the water. Anyone involved in an extreme career must always think ahead, plan carefully, prepare well, and be mindful of safety concerns. Following these guidelines increases the chance of extreme success in the professional scuba diving world.

Glossary

bell saturation diver   Diver who sinks to great depths inside an atmospherically controlled metal object

bends   Health condition that arises when divers ascend to the surface of the water too quickly, causing nitrogen bubbles to lodge painfully in the joints.

C-card   Certification required to legally dive without an instructor present.

commercial air diver   Performer of underwater repairs, inspections, and construction tasks on oil rigs and bridges.

decompression chamber   A small room where divers have simulated seawater pressure applied to their bodies to alleviate the bends.

dive buddy   A diver's partner who is responsible for helping out if problems arise on a dive.

dive computer   Waterproof computer that helps divers avoid the bends by gauging information like water depth, time spent under water, and water temperature.

dive instructor   Teacher of the necessities of diving.

dive resort   Lush, tropical haven where divers can stay and enjoy guided diving expeditions.

diver medic   Medic who administers first aid and CPR on a dive site.

diver physician   Doctor specially trained to handle diving-related injuries and health problems.

diving journalist   Writer of feature stories for diving magazines, and diving stories for mainstream publications.

marine biologist   Scientist who studies undersea animals and how they fit into the marine environment.

nitrox   A special type of air some divers breathe that contains less nitrogen than normal air.

police search-and-recovery teams   Divers hired by the police to search for evidence of crimes.

rapture of the deep   An illness caused by diving ninety feet deep or more.

regulator   Device that regulates air between a diver's air tank and mouth.

Scuba Divers: Life Under Water

resort dive guide   The leader of diving expeditions at dive resorts.

ROV (remotely operated vehicle) technician   Operator of underwater robotics.

salvage diver   Diver who recovers treasure, cargo, and other materials that go down with a shipwreck.

scuba (self-contained underwater breathing apparatus)   A diver's equipment.

underwater archaeologist   Diver who searches for and examines shipwrecks for the purpose of scientific study.

underwater cinematographer   Diver who is hired to film underwater sequences for television and film.

underwater photographer   Diver skilled at taking photographs of the undersea world.

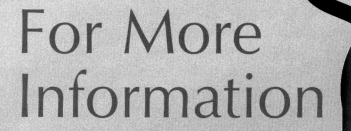

For More Information

In the United States

Center for Marine Conservation
1725 DeSales Street NW
Suite 600
Washington, DC 20036
(202) 429-5609
Web site: http://www.cmc-ocean.org

Divers Alert Network (DAN)
The Peter B. Bennett Center
6 West Colony Place
Durham, NC 27705
(800) 446-2671
Web site: http://www.diversalertnetwork.org

Greenpeace
702 H Street NW
Washington, DC 20001
(800) 326-0959
Web site: http://www.greenpeaceusa.org

National Association of
   Underwater Instructors (NAUI)
P.O. Box 89789
Tampa, FL 33689-0413
(800) 553-6284
Web site: http://www.naui.org

National Oceanic and
   Atmospheric Administration (NOAA)
14th Street and Constitution Avenue NW
Room 6013
Washington, DC 20230
(202) 482-6090
Web site: http://www.noaa.gov

National YMCA Scuba Program
5825-2A Live Oak Parkway

Norcross, GA 30093-1728
(888) 464-9622
Web site: http://www.ymcascuba.org

Oceanic Society
Fort Mason Center, Building E
San Francisco, CA 94123
(800) 326-7491
Web site: http://www.oceanic-society.org

Professional Association of Diving Instructors (PADI)
30151 Tomas Street
Rancho Santa Margarita, CA 92688-2125
(800) 729-7234
Web site: http://www.padi.com

Scuba Schools International (SSI)
2619 Canton Court
Fort Collins, CO 80525-4498
(970) 482-0883
Web site: http://www.ssiusa.com

In Canada

Professional Association of Diving Instructors (PADI)
3771 Jacombs Road
Building C #535
Richmond, BC V6V 2L9
(800) 565-8130
Web site: http://www.padi.com

Technical Diving International (TDI) Canada
141-5 Hotchkiss Street
Gravenhurst, ON P1P 1H6
(705) 687-9226
Web site: http://www.tdicanada.com

For Further Reading

Ballard, Robert D, and Rick Archbold. *The Lost Wreck of the Isis.* New York: Scholastic, 1990.

Blot, Jean-Yves. *Underwater Archaeology: Exploring the World Beneath the Sea.* New York: Abrams, 1996.

Cussler, Clive, and Craig Dirgo. *The Sea Hunters.* New York: Simon & Schuster, 1996.

Divers Alert Network. *Medical Requirements for Scuba Divers.* Durham, NC: DAN, 1989.

Edge, Martin. *The Underwater Photographer.* 2nd ed. Boston: Focal Press, 1999.

Lang, Denise V. *Footsteps in the Ocean: Careers in Diving.* New York: Dutton, 1987.

Levinton, Jeffrey S. *Marine Biology: Function, Biodiversity, Ecology.* 2nd ed. New York: Oxford University Press, 2001.

Maas, Peter. *The Terrible Hours: The Man Behind the Greatest Submarine Rescue in History*. New York: HarperCollins Publishers, 1999.

Professional Association of Diving Instructors. *The Encyclopedia of Recreational Diving*. Rancho Santa Margarita, CA: PADI, 1998.

Index

About the Author

John Giacobello is a freelance writer living in New York City. He is also the author of *Choosing a Career in Music* and *Exploring Careers in the Fashion Industry*.

Photo Credits

Cover © Jonathan Blair/Corbis; p. 7 courtesy of www.divingheritage; pp. 12, 18, 30 © Jonathan Blair/Corbis; p.14 © Jeffery L. Rotman/Corbis; p. 23 © Associated Press AP; p. 26 © Amos Nachoum/Corbis; p. 37 © AP/Citizen's Voice; p. 39 © Tim Wright/Corbis; p. 43 © The Purcell Team/Corbis; p. 47 The Everett Collection; p. 48 Cindy Reiman.

Design and Layout

Les Kanturek